KU-034-670

LOOKING AT HOW ANIMALS LIVE
MONKEYS AND APES

Published 1986 by
Hamlyn Publishing
a division of The Hamlyn Publishing Group Limited
Bridge House, London Road,
Twickenham, Middlesex, England

Copyright ©1986 Ilex Publishers Limited

All rights reserved. No part of this publication may be
reproduced, stored in a retrieval system, or transmitted
in any form or by any means, electronic, mechanical,
photocopying, recording or otherwise, without the
permission of Hamlyn Publishing and the copyright holder.

ISBN 0 600 53025 6

Typesetting by Thomas/Weintroub Associates, London
Colour separations by Trilogy, Milan
Printed in Italy

Created and produced by Ilex Publishers Ltd.,
29-31 George Street, Oxford OX1 2AJ, in association
with Linden Artists Ltd., 86 Petty France, London SW1H 9EA.

Illustrated by Martin Camm/Linden Artists

LOOKING AT HOW ANIMALS LIVE
MONKEYS AND APES

Written by Mark Carwardine
Illustrated by Martin Camm

HAMLYN

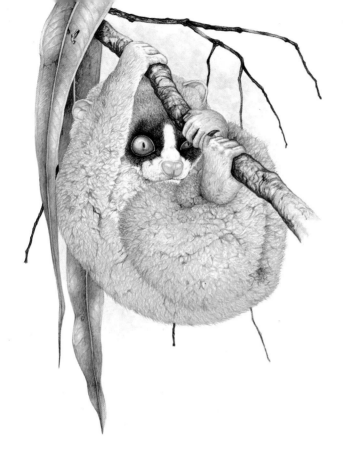

This series is dedicated to Georgia, aged 7 who
showed us how children look at animals

CONTENTS

Aye-Aye

The aye-aye looks like a strange creature from outer-space. It has rat-like teeth, a bushy, squirrel-like tail, a cat-like body, and huge eyes and ears. In fact, scientists spent over 100 years trying to identify it.

Aye-ayes are extremely rare animals. They live in some of the rain forests on the east coast of Madagascar, where they are active only at night. The daytime is spent sleeping in ball-shaped nests made of leaves and branches, but they wake up and start moving around as soon as the sun goes down.

Aye-ayes travel through the trees easily and jump about like lemurs and monkeys. They even hang upside-down, using their claws as hooks to cling onto branches.

Their favourite food is grubs, which live under the bark of trees. The aye-aye carefully places one of its ears next to the bark, listening for the slightest sounds of the tiny animals. Then it quickly gnaws a hole into the tree and pulls out the grubs with its long, thin, middle finger which looks like a bent twig. Most aye-ayes make grunting noises when they are eating.

If you get too close to one of these strange animals, it hisses or makes a 'ha-hay' call by blowing through its nose. This is given only as a warning, to frighten off intruders, but most human tribes in Madagascar are scared stiff by the noise.

Gorilla

Despite its great strength and impressive chest-beating displays, the gorilla is no more savage than any other wild animal. In fact, it is docile and friendly and is only dangerous when threatened or harmed.

Gorillas are the largest of all monkeys and apes. They can be taller than a man — and are often twice as heavy. Very rare animals, they live in small groups, or families, in the jungles of central Africa. Most of their time is spent on the ground, eating wild celery, roots, tree bark and many other kinds of plant material. They do sometimes climb trees, usually to look for food or to get a bird's eye view of their forest homes. They sometimes build sleeping nests there, of branches and leaves.

They feed during the morning and evening, but take a rest for a few hours at mid-day, when they love to sunbathe.

Young gorillas, however, spend a great deal of their time playing. They climb trees, slide down tree trunks, wrestle with each other, swing on branches, play chasing games and even irritate the adults in the troop. Just like human children! But these playtimes are important in their growing-up. They enable the young gorillas to copy what their parents do, and to learn how to climb, find food and do other things.

Chimpanzee

Chimpanzees, which live in the jungles and grasslands of Africa, are very similar and closely related to people. They often hold hands when they are together; they kiss when they meet; and can even smile, or look worried if something is troubling them.

They are also very intelligent animals. Unlike most other monkeys and apes they are able to use tools. For example, they lower sticks into ants' nests, wait for the ants to crawl up, then sweep them into their mouths before

they have time to bite. They also use sticks or rocks to smash open fruit with hard shells — or throw them to frighten off leopards and other enemies. They have even been known to use leaves like sponges, by dipping them in water and then washing with them.

Chimpanzees eat mainly fruit, young leaves, seeds and flowers, but will also take honey, eggs, caterpillars, birds and anything else they can get their hands on. On occasion, they even eat small monkeys, pigs and antelopes. They live in 'chimpanzee towns' which consist of fifty or more chimps, but usually feed and wander on their own. If one of them, however, finds a lot of food it barks excitedly to announce the good news to its friends. Then they all rush over to join in the feast, grunting softly to show that they are pleased and contented.

Although chimpanzees spend much of their time on the ground, they climb into the trees after dark to sleep. Each night they build a new leafy nest, especially for the purpose, in branches about ten metres above the ground.

Orang-utan

Very loud grumbling and burbling sounds can sometimes be heard in the jungles of Sumatra and Borneo, two islands in Indonesia. They are made by one of our long-haired relatives, the orang-utan.

Orangs spend most of their time swinging from branch to branch high up in the trees. Their arms are very strong and are so long that when they stand upright their fingers almost touch the ground.

Orang-utans always rise early in the morning and spend the rest of the day searching for food. They eat mostly fruit and leaves, but sometimes choose flowers, bark and insects. Their favourite food of all is wild figs. At midday, they usually have a nap, covering their forehead and eyes with their hands, and then continue eating until it begins to get dark.

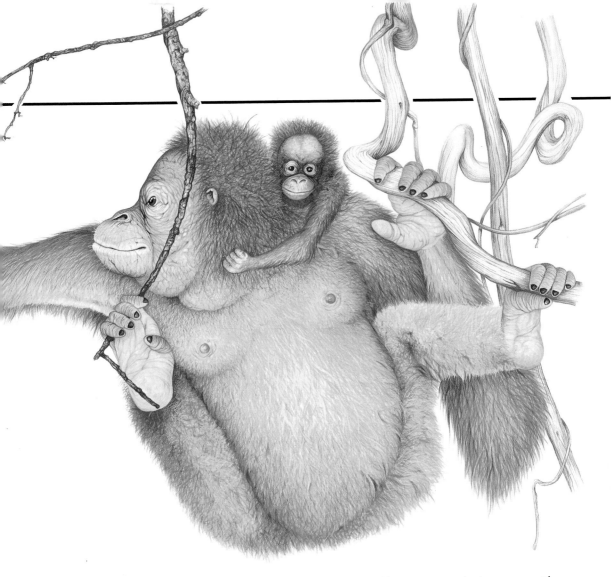

Every night, orangs build a special sleeping nest in the trees out of leaves and branches. Sometimes, if it is raining, they will even build a roof — or hold big leaves and branches over their heads to protect themselves — just as people use umbrellas!

Baby orang-utans often ride on their mother's back and will stay with her until they are about six or seven years old. Then they will be able to look after themselves.

But loggers and farmers are cutting down enormous areas of jungle, meaning that orangs have fewer places to roam and find food than they once did. So these days they are very rare.

Ring-tailed Lemur

Ring-tailed lemurs can leap easily from tree to tree but they do not feel as safe, high in the air, as other lemurs or monkeys. They prefer strong and wide branches to the thin and dangerous ones their relatives often use. Best of all, they like to have their feet firmly on the ground.

Ring-tailed lemurs live in the forests and scrubby areas of southern Madagascar. They are easily recognised by their black and white tails, which are always held in the air in the shape of a question-mark when they are walking or running along the ground. They use their tails like flags, to show their companions exactly where they are.

Up to twenty or more lemurs live together in one troop. They often purr when they are together, just like cats, and will even miaow if they get separated from their friends. Other calls they make include a yap or a scream, if a dangerous animal like a snake or a hawk is nearby, and a howling call which sounds rather like a wolf.

Most of the ring-tailed lemur's day is spent foraging for food — mostly fruit, but also leaves and, occasionally, insects. The animals take only a short nap at midday and are sometimes active after dark as well. They have very good eyesight — and can see well in dim light — but rely more on their fox-like noses. Smells are sometimes used to frighten off unwelcome lemurs in the troop or visiting lemurs from other troops. They dip their tails in special scent glands on their wrists and shiver them at one another during long 'stink fights'.

Tree Shrew

Living in the jungles of south-east Asia is an animal that looks nothing like either a monkey or an ape. With a large bushy tail, it looks more like a long-nosed squirrel. But squirrels have long whiskers and this animal, a tree shrew, does not. Instead, it is believed by many scientists to be closely-related to monkeys because it has very similar teeth and a similar skull. Monkeys may even have looked like tree shrews many millions of years ago.

Like both squirrels and monkeys, tree shrews are good climbers and are as happy in the trees as they are on the ground. Active throughout the day, they leave their shelters at dawn and return in plenty of time before sunset. They are constantly on the move and busy searching for their favourite food, insects and fruit. Sometimes they hold the food in their hands and sit down comfortably before eating it.

Tree shrews breed at virtually any time of year. Up to three young are born in a tree hollow lined with dry leaves. The young animals are visited and fed by their mother only once every two days for the first five weeks or so of their lives. Then they begin to emerge from their hollow tree and move over to their parents' nest to sleep at night. They grow so rapidly after the move that they are the same size as their parents within just a few months.

Gibbon

Gibbons are the acrobats of the animal world. They spend nearly all their lives swinging in the trees and almost never come to the ground. Sometimes they even walk upright on dangerous-looking branches — with their arms out to keep balance — just like circus tightrope walkers.

18

Normally, in their jungle homes of southern Asia, gibbons move around at a leisurely pace. But they can swing with incredible speed when they want to and can even catch small birds in mid-air. They hurl themselves enormous distances into space, grab an isolated branch and swing off again, using their hands as hooks. Indeed, gibbons can move faster than any of the other monkeys and apes. Sometimes, though, they do make mistakes and most gibbons break a bone or two at some time in their lives.

Every morning when they wake up they sing loudly to tell other gibbons to stay away from their homes, which are guarded enthusiastically. If an intruder does come too close they hoot loudly to frighten it away.

Sometimes two gibbons will sing together, in a loud and joyful duet, for as long as fifteen minutes every day. But they are very unpredictable animals. They may be singing happily, and be loving and friendly, one minute — but the next they could burst into a tantrum and start smashing branches — for no apparent reason.

Black and White Colobus Monkey

If you look up to the tops of the trees in Africa's jungles you may be lucky enough to see long tails with white fluffy tufts on the ends, dangling through the leaves. They belong to black and white colobus monkeys, which really are a spectacular black and white in colour. They take special care to groom their coats and spend hours cleaning and looking after their tail tufts.

Most common in trees along jungle rivers, they live in small groups of about eight. They are usually friendly animals but, when two groups meet, there is much chasing and fighting, as well as arm-waving, calling and leaping about. They have special dawn choruses every day, when adult males sing loudly, specifically to warn other groups to stay away. All in all, they are very noisy animals and the only time they really stay very quiet is during bad weather, which they do not like at all.

Black and white colobus monkeys live high up in the forest canopy. The only times they come nearer to the ground are when a hawk or eagle flies over and they have to flee to safety, or if the trees are too far apart for them to

jump. They can make fantastic leaps from tree to tree, using branches like elastic bands and catapulting themselves into the air. They land feet first among the foliage with a tremendous crash. The young colobus monkeys, which are completely white, can leap from tree to tree when only about six months old.

Bushbaby

In the middle of the night, deep in the forests and shrublands of Africa, you sometimes hear strange sounds, just like human babies crying in their cots. But the noises are not made by people at all. They are made by bushbabies, whose loud calls really do sound like human children.

There are several different kinds of bushbaby, ranging in size from that of a squirrel to almost as big as a cat. They are all expert jumpers and make flying leaps to travel from tree to tree. Each time they jump they tuck their arms and legs

Bushbabies come out at night to feed on tree gum, insects, lizards, mice and small birds. At first, very young ones are 'parked' on a branch while their mothers search for food. When they are old enough they prefer to follow her around, though they often have to make clicking calls for her to return or slow down because they cannot keep up.

tightly against their bodies in mid-air. They can jump as far as five metres in one leap and, during their travels, can cover several kilometres in a single night. They also have special suckers on their fingers and toes to help them cling to the trees.

Bushbabies have big eyes, for seeing in the dark, and very sensitive ears. Even the slightest sound will not escape their keen sense of hearing. But when they are asleep, during the day and in a nest of leaves and twigs, their large ears get in the way — so they fold them up before settling down.

Potto

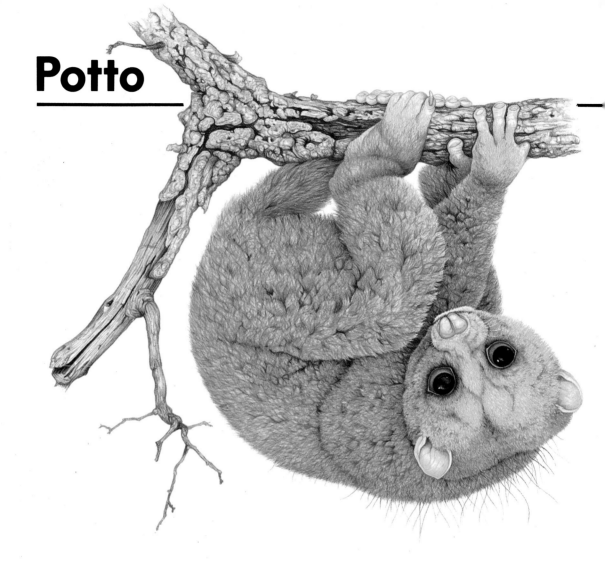

Pottos are tough little animals and can defend themselves from most enemies by biting with their sharp teeth. But they rarely fight in the wild and prefer to stay motionless in the hope of not being seen; or, if they are in great danger, they simply let go and fall to the ground.

About the size of large squirrels, pottos live in the trees, particularly around forest clearings, in central and western Africa. They are active only at night when they climb very slowly and carefully, letting go with one foot

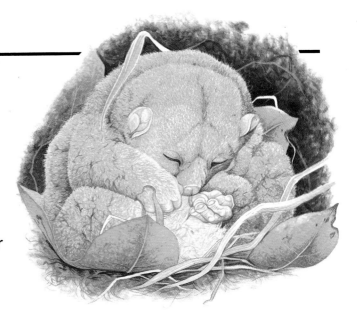

only when the other three have a firm grip on the branch. Very occasionally, they dare to rear on to their hind legs to catch moths in flight. They never leap or jump but can travel along upside-down as readily as on top, and sometimes even sleep hanging underneath the branches.

It is more common, however, for them to shelter by day in hollow trees, curled up into tight woolly balls.

Pottos feed on fruit, tree gum, insects, small birds, bats, mice and snails. Their keen noses and eyes help them to find food easily in the dark — but they only actually eat once every two days. One young potto is born each year.

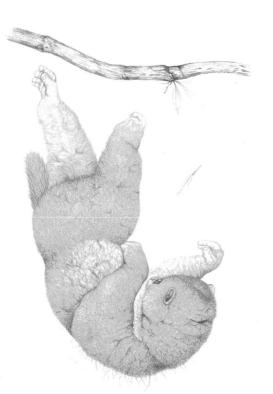

Howler Monkey

In the huge trees of South America's rain forests lives the noisiest monkey in the world, the howler monkey. Its cries and howls can be heard up to five kilometres away. The sound is rather like a lion's roar and helps to keep other howler monkeys, in neighbouring groups, away from their favourite trees.

Usually about ten howler monkeys live together, though sometimes there may be as many as fifty in a single group. They spend a great deal of the day and all of the night resting, but get up and move around to look for food, which is mostly leaves and fruit, whenever they feel hungry. Although they sleep in places low down the trees, nearer the ground, they move up to near the roof of the jungle early every morning, to sing and start the day's work of finding food.

Howler monkeys have very long and flexible tails, which act rather like extra arms and even allow them to hang from branches upside-down.

This is useful because it leaves their hands and feet free for eating. In fact, their tails are so strong that, if the monkeys make a mistake when climbing and fall, they can use them to catch a branch on the way down. This is why very few howler monkeys fall and actually hit the ground.

Spider Monkey

If you are walking through the jungles of South America and dead branches start falling on top of you, do not be surprised. They are probably being thrown by spider monkeys, hiding in the tree tops. If you get too close to their trees they shake the branches excitedly and make threatening growls to frighten you away. However, all this is bluff to scare potential enemies; spider monkeys are not very courageous animals and will slip away and hide if any enemy persists and the situation begins to look dangerous.

They are almost as acrobatic as gibbons and move swiftly through the trees, particularly in the small branches right at the top. Their long and flexible tails are very useful and act as an extra arm, even being able to pick up small objects.

Spider monkeys live in groups of up to about thirty, though individuals come and go as they please. They are very noisy animals and emit terrier-like barks or make strange sounds like the whinnying of a horse. Fruit is their favourite food, but they also eat nuts, seeds, buds, flowers, leaves, spiders, and birds' eggs.

Most feeding takes place very early in the morning and the monkeys rest for the remainder of the day.

Mandrill

The mandrill is not only the largest of all monkeys — it is also one of the most colourful. It has blue cheeks, an incredible red nose and a yellow chin. Most other monkeys and apes are fairly dull in comparison.

When a mandrill gets excited all the colours become even brighter. Its chest turns bright blue and red spots appear on its wrists and ankles. These changes all act as signals, rather like a special kind of language without words. But they do speak to one another as well. When they get cross they often act like spoilt children; they grunt, chatter, shake their heads and even angrily slap the ground with their hands. They can be very vicious and sometimes kill other animals when they get really angry.

Mandrills live in groups of up to fifty or more, in the jungles of West Africa. The large adults spend most of their time on the ground, while the smaller females and young animals live in the trees.

Towards the end of the afternoon, in preparation for the night, they all climb up into the trees to sleep. Mandrills often roam great distances, even though they always take a rest at mid-day, in search of food such as fruit, nuts, small animals and even snakes.

Baboon

Baboons spend most of the day on the ground but, for safety reasons, they move high up into the trees, or onto rocky cliffs, at night. On the ground they are in danger from lions, leopards, cheetahs, wild dogs and other predators. If they are unfortunate enough to meet one of these dangerous animals they attempt to run away, but adult male baboons will often try to defend the troop. They are powerful and fierce fighters with their large, sharp teeth.

There are several different kinds of baboon. They all live and travel in tightly organised troops, sometimes numbering several hundred individuals. First thing in the morning, however, they usually split up into smaller groups to forage.

Baboons are the largest of all monkeys. They live almost everywhere in Africa where they can find drinking water, usually choosing rocky, open countryside or forest edges to make their homes.

Each group may travel as far as twenty kilometres a day looking for food, which includes plants, roots, insects and other small animals. In areas such as South Africa, where they live along the coast, they will also eat crabs and other seashore creatures. When they are feeding, they typically stand on three legs and pluck their food with their free hand.

Young baboons can be born at any time of the year. After they are about a week old they begin to ride on their mothers' backs, clinging on like a jockey on a horse.

Mouse Lemur

The mouse lemur is one of the smallest of all monkeys and apes. It lives in the jungles of Madagascar and spends most of its time in the trees, only coming down to the ground to cross large gaps or to catch beetles, spiders and frogs. In the trees, fruit and other small animals are eaten as well.

Baby mouse lemurs are only about three or four centimetres long. Two or three of them are born in a nest of leaves or a hollow tree. As soon as they are born their mother holds them in her hands and spends hours licking them clean. They never travel on her back like other lemurs or monkeys; instead, the mother carries them around in her mouth. After about three weeks, though, they are already good climbers and are acquiring impressive skills in running and jumping. The tiny animals play lots of games at first but within only two months they look and behave just like their parents. They are able to

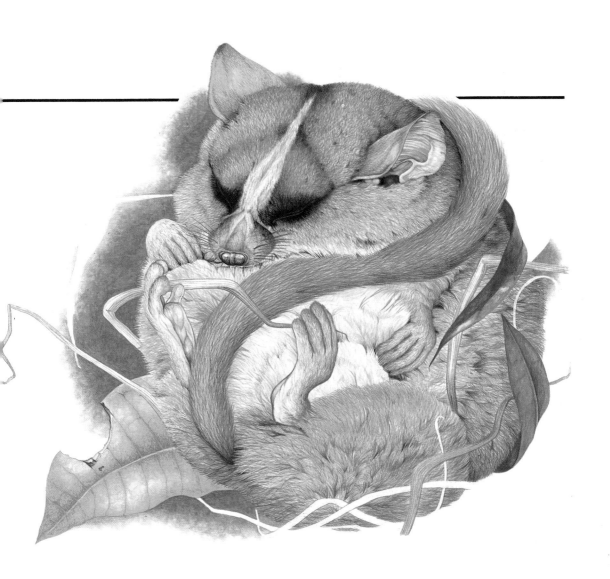

have young of their own when they are just one year old.

Mouse lemurs feed alone at night but they like to stay fairly close to others of their kind. They keep in contact in the dark by regularly calling to one another. Although they are active for much of the year, during the dry season they rest or hibernate in a hollow tree. They eat virtually nothing and go completely stiff until the rains return.

Indri

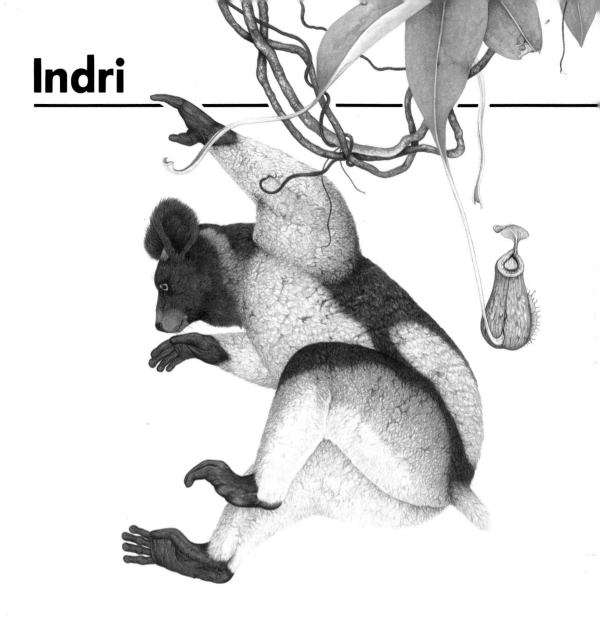

The indri makes the loudest noise of any animal in Madagascar. It sounds like a mixture of a dog howling and a person crying in pain — and can be very spooky. Every morning, soon after daybreak, lots of indris get together and sing as loudly as they can. It is an ear-deafening start to the jungle's day.

Indris are very rare animals, found only in a few jungles on the slopes of volcanoes in Madagascar. They are large black-and-white lemurs with long eyelashes. Many centuries ago, there were indris around that grew so big they were even taller than a man, but today they average a little under a metre from head to foot.

Living high up in the tree tops, in family groups, indris eat mostly leaves and fruit. Occasionally, they will come down to the ground to eat earth, which is supposed to help with their digestion, but most of the time they prefer to stay in the safety of the trees. They are very much at home in the upper branches, high above the ground, and are such powerful leapers that they seem to bounce from tree to tree, sometimes leaping up to ten metres in one go.

Young indris are born in May and travel around on their mothers' backs, like baby baboons and other monkeys and apes.

Slow Loris

Very few people have been lucky enough to see a slow loris in the wild. It is a secretive animal, only coming out at night and spending most of its time hidden from sight in the trees.

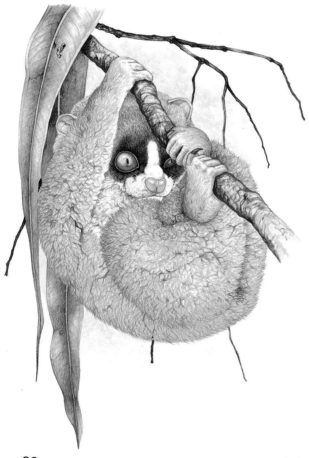

Slow lorises live in the jungles and bamboo forests of Asia. They never seem to be in a hurry and move almost in slow motion, rather like a chameleon or a sloth. They seem quite nervous about falling off their branches and cling on really tightly, never lifting more than one hand or foot at a time. In fact, if they are really determined to cling on, slow lorises are almost impossible to budge, no matter how much you tug and pull. They never seem to get tired; they can even hang upside-down by their feet, for hours on end, while eating with their hands.

Slow lorises eat fruit, snails, insects, lizards, birds and other small animals. For such slow movers they can strike their prey with incredible speed. Likewise, they can leap forward suddenly and give a quick, painful bite if you try to touch them or get too close.

Unlike many of their relatives, slow lorises do not build nests for their young. Instead, the babies are born in the open and then carried around by their mothers; sometimes they are even left clinging desperately to a branch while the adults forage for food.

Proboscis Monkey

The proboscis monkey is the elephant of the monkeys and apes. It has an enormous nose — sometimes over seven centimetres long — which hangs down over its mouth and almost touches its chin. This strange contraption is used as a loudspeaker for the animal's warning honk, which sounds rather like a noisy goose and can be heard some distance

away. Only the males have long noses, which swell or become red when they get angry or excited, in much the same way as people blush when they are embarrassed.
The females have smaller noses and make milder calls, while the young animals have turned-up noses.

They may be ugly — but proboscis monkeys are also friendly and peaceful. They live around the mangrove swamps and riverbanks of Borneo, an island in south-east Asia. Most of their time is spent sunbathing in the trees, often gathering in groups of twenty or more. But towards the end of the afternoon they become more active and start feeding on leaves and mangrove shoots. In fact, they can be surprisingly agile and can leap up to eight metres from branch to branch when they want to.

Proboscis monkeys are also excellent swimmers and can swim as well under the water as on the surface. Sometimes they do spectacular dives from branches high above and enter the water with an enormous splash.

Japanese Macaque

Japanese macaques are astonishingly like people in many ways. They learn very quickly and are able to teach one another different tricks and techniques. They are even able to walk on two legs, carrying their food in their arms as they go.

During very bad winters, Japanese macaques keep themselves warm by taking regular hot baths. They have learned that the warm water from volcanic springs is ideal for sitting in, to keep out of the cold and for protection from snowstorms and blizzards. Only their heads stick out of the water and these often get covered with snow — which sometimes sits several centimetres thick on top!

The only problem with taking baths is that the macaques have to clamber out of the springs to search for food. The temperatures outside are often well below freezing and the snow can be over a metre deep. The poor animals must get very cold, especially when their long and shaggy coats are soaking wet.

Japanese macaques are big monkeys which live in very large troops; up to seven hundred of them have been seen together. They live high up in the mountains of Japan. Although they are excellent climbers, they spend most of their time on the ground, bathing or searching for fruit, leaves, insects or other small animals to eat. Some of them wash their food in water, others dip it in the sea because they like the salty taste.

Golden Lion Tamarin

A spectacular golden colour all over, the golden lion tamarin really does look like a small lion. It is one of the most strikingly-coloured of all monkeys and apes.

It is also one of the rarest. There may be fewer than a hundred golden lion tamarins surviving in the wild, in only two areas of jungle on the coastal mountains of Brazil.

People are cutting down their forest homes and even capture the animals for sale as pets or to zoos. Sometimes they are eaten by the South American people living nearby. If nothing is done to protect them from all these hazards, golden lion tamarins could become extinct in the wild by the end of the century.

These small monkeys leap or jump with unbelievable speed from branch to branch. Their long fingers help them hold on to a branch after particularly long jumps and therefore prevent them from falling.

Normally quite gentle animals, golden lion tamarins live happily in groups of up to eight at a time. However, they can be quite aggressive, threatening other tamarins, or even people, by erecting their manes, showing their teeth and emitting shrill and very high shrieking sounds. They eat fruit, flowers, frogs, lizards, snails, insects, tree gum and nectar.